Write, Heal, Thrive Journaling Series Volume 1
Developed by Melissa B. Lombardo
Illustrated by Eduardo José Arias Cruz

write
heal
thrive

Copyright Notice

Publisher Note

Contact

For permission requests, quantity sales, special discounts, production and licensing assistance, speaking engagements, and workshops, contact the author at: info@melissablombardo.com.

Publisher's Cataloging-in-Publication Data Write, Heal, Thrive Journaling Series by Melissa B. Lombardo. First Edition.

1. Self Help

2. Personal Transformation

3. Journals

Written by Melissa B. Lombardo.

Cover illustration by Eduardo José Arias Cruz.
   eduardoariascruz.com

Layout and logo designed by Nikita Prokhorov.
   nikitaprokhorov.com

Printed in the United States of America

Publisher information: Write, Heal, Thrive, West Hartford, CT.

ISBN 979-8-9877587-5-5 (Paperback)

Other Works by Melissa Lombardo

Hurt, Healing, and Hope: Thriving beyond Sexual Assault

Write, Heal, Thrive: A Transformative Journaling Experience

This Journal belongs to: / Este Diario pertenece a:

You Matter!
¡Tu eres importante!

Now Get Ready to Write, Heal, and Thrive.
¡Ahora prepárate para escribir, sanar, y triunfar.

Journal

Journal *(Continued)*

Journal *(Continued)*

Journal *(Continued)*

Journal *(Continued)*

Journal *(Continued)*

Journal *(Continued)*

_____

_____

_____

_____

_____

_____

_____

_____

_____

_____

_____

_____

_____

_____

_____

_____

_____

_____

_____

_____

_____

_____

_____

_____

_____

Journal *(Continued)*

Journal *(Continued)*

_____

_____

_____

_____

_____

_____

_____

_____

_____

_____

_____

_____

_____

_____

_____

_____

_____

_____

_____

_____

_____

_____

_____

_____

_____

Journal *(Continued)*

Journal *(Continued)*

_____

_____

_____

_____

_____

_____

_____

_____

_____

_____

_____

_____

_____

_____

_____

_____

_____

_____

_____

_____

_____

_____

_____

_____

_____

_____

_____

Journal *(Continued)*

Journal *(Continued)*

_____

_____

_____

_____

_____

_____

_____

_____

_____

_____

_____

_____

_____

_____

_____

_____

_____

_____

_____

_____

_____

_____

_____

_____

_____

_____

_____

_____

Journal *(Continued)*

Journal *(Continued)*

_____

_____

_____

_____

_____

_____

_____

_____

_____

_____

_____

_____

_____

_____

_____

_____

_____

_____

_____

_____

_____

_____

_____

_____

_____

_____

Journal *(Continued)*

Journal *(Continued)*

_____

_____

_____

_____

_____

_____

_____

_____

_____

_____

_____

_____

_____

_____

_____

_____

_____

_____

_____

_____

_____

_____

_____

_____

_____

_____

Journal *(Continued)*

_____

_____

_____

_____

_____

_____

_____

_____

_____

_____

_____

_____

_____

_____

_____

_____

_____

_____

_____

_____

_____

_____

_____

_____

_____

_____

_____

_____

_____

_____

_____

Journal *(Continued)*

Journal *(Continued)*

_____

_____

_____

_____

_____

_____

_____

_____

_____

_____

_____

_____

_____

_____

_____

_____

_____

_____

_____

_____

_____

_____

_____

_____

_____

_____

_____

_____

Journal *(Continued)*

Journal *(Continued)*

_____

_____

_____

_____

_____

_____

_____

_____

_____

_____

_____

_____

_____

_____

_____

_____

_____

_____

_____

_____

_____

_____

_____

_____

_____

_____

_____

_____

Journal *(Continued)*

_____

_____

_____

_____

_____

_____

_____

_____

_____

_____

_____

_____

_____

_____

_____

_____

_____

_____

_____

_____

_____

_____

_____

_____

_____

Journal *(Continued)*

_____

_____

_____

_____

_____

_____

_____

_____

_____

_____

_____

_____

_____

_____

_____

_____

_____

_____

_____

_____

_____

_____

_____

_____

_____

Journal *(Continued)*

Journal *(Continued)*

Journal *(Continued)*

_____

_____

_____

_____

_____

_____

_____

_____

_____

_____

_____

_____

_____

_____

_____

_____

_____

_____

_____

_____

_____

_____

_____

_____

_____

Journal *(Continued)*

Journal *(Continued)*

Journal *(Continued)*

Journal *(Continued)*

_____

_____

_____

_____

_____

_____

_____

_____

_____

_____

_____

_____

_____

_____

_____

_____

_____

_____

_____

_____

_____

_____

_____

_____

_____

_____

_____

_____

_____

Journal *(Continued)*

Journal *(Continued)*

Journal *(Continued)*

Journal *(Continued)*

Journal *(Continued)*

Journal *(Continued)*

_____

_____

_____

_____

_____

_____

_____

_____

_____

_____

_____

_____

_____

_____

_____

_____

_____

_____

_____

_____

_____

_____

_____

_____

_____

_____

Journal *(Continued)*

_____

_____

_____

_____

_____

_____

_____

_____

_____

_____

_____

_____

_____

_____

_____

_____

_____

_____

_____

_____

_____

_____

_____

_____

_____

Journal *(Continued)*

Journal *(Continued)*

_____

_____

_____

_____

_____

_____

_____

_____

_____

_____

_____

_____

_____

_____

_____

_____

_____

_____

_____

_____

_____

_____

_____

_____

_____

_____

_____

_____

_____

Journal *(Continued)*

Journal *(Continued)*

Journal *(Continued)*

Journal *(Continued)*

Journal *(Continued)*

Journal *(Continued)*

Journal *(Continued)*

_____

_____

_____

_____

_____

_____

_____

_____

_____

_____

_____

_____

_____

_____

_____

_____

_____

_____

_____

_____

_____

_____

_____

_____

Journal *(Continued)*

Journal *(Continued)*

_____

_____

_____

_____

_____

_____

_____

_____

_____

_____

_____

_____

_____

_____

_____

_____

_____

_____

_____

_____

_____

_____

_____

_____

Journal *(Continued)*

Journal *(Continued)*

_____

_____

_____

_____

_____

_____

_____

_____

_____

_____

_____

_____

_____

_____

_____

_____

_____

_____

_____

_____

_____

_____

_____

_____

_____

Journal *(Continued)*

Journal *(Continued)*

_____

_____

_____

_____

_____

_____

_____

_____

_____

_____

_____

_____

_____

_____

_____

_____

_____

_____

_____

_____

_____

_____

_____

_____

_____

Journal *(Continued)*

Journal *(Continued)*

_____

_____

_____

_____

_____

_____

_____

_____

_____

_____

_____

_____

_____

_____

_____

_____

_____

_____

_____

_____

_____

_____

_____

_____

_____

Journal *(Continued)*

_____

_____

_____

_____

_____

_____

_____

_____

_____

_____

_____

_____

_____

_____

_____

_____

_____

_____

_____

_____

_____

_____

_____

_____

_____

Journal *(Continued)*

_____

_____

_____

_____

_____

_____

_____

_____

_____

_____

_____

_____

_____

_____

_____

_____

_____

_____

_____

_____

_____

_____

_____

_____

_____

_____

_____

_____

_____

Journal *(Continued)*

Journal *(Continued)*

Journal *(Continued)*

Journal *(Continued)*

Journal *(Continued)*

Journal *(Continued)*

Journal *(Continued)*

Journal *(Continued)*

Journal *(Continued)*

Journal *(Continued)*

Journal *(Continued)*

Journal *(Continued)*

_____

_____

_____

_____

_____

_____

_____

_____

_____

_____

_____

_____

_____

_____

_____

_____

_____

_____

_____

_____

_____

_____

_____

_____

_____

Journal *(Continued)*

Journal *(Continued)*

_____

_____

_____

_____

_____

_____

_____

_____

_____

_____

_____

_____

_____

_____

_____

_____

_____

_____

_____

_____

_____

_____

_____

_____

_____

_____

_____

Journal *(Continued)*

_____

_____

_____

_____

_____

_____

_____

_____

_____

_____

_____

_____

_____

_____

_____

_____

_____

_____

_____

_____

_____

_____

_____

_____

_____

_____

Journal *(Continued)*

_____

_____

_____

_____

_____

_____

_____

_____

_____

_____

_____

_____

_____

_____

_____

_____

_____

_____

_____

_____

_____

_____

_____

_____

_____

_____

_____

_____

Journal *(Continued)*

Journal *(Continued)*

Journal *(Continued)*

Journal *(Continued)*

_____

_____

_____

_____

_____

_____

_____

_____

_____

_____

_____

_____

_____

_____

_____

_____

_____

_____

_____

_____

_____

_____

_____

_____

Journal *(Continued)*

Journal *(Continued)*

_____

_____

_____

_____

_____

_____

_____

_____

_____

_____

_____

_____

_____

_____

_____

_____

_____

_____

_____

_____

_____

_____

_____

_____

_____

_____

Journal *(Continued)*

_____

_____

_____

_____

_____

_____

_____

_____

_____

_____

_____

_____

_____

_____

_____

_____

_____

_____

_____

_____

_____

_____

_____

_____

_____

_____

_____

_____

Journal *(Continued)*

_____

_____

_____

_____

_____

_____

_____

_____

_____

_____

_____

_____

_____

_____

_____

_____

_____

_____

_____

_____

_____

_____

_____

_____

_____

_____

Journal *(Continued)*

_____

_____

_____

_____

_____

_____

_____

_____

_____

_____

_____

_____

_____

_____

_____

_____

_____

_____

_____

_____

_____

_____

_____

_____

_____

_____

Journal *(Continued)*

_____

_____

_____

_____

_____

_____

_____

_____

_____

_____

_____

_____

_____

_____

_____

_____

_____

_____

_____

_____

_____

_____

_____

_____

_____

_____

_____

_____

Journal *(Continued)*

Journal *(Continued)*

_____

_____

_____

_____

_____

_____

_____

_____

_____

_____

_____

_____

_____

_____

_____

_____

_____

_____

_____

_____

_____

_____

_____

_____

_____

_____

_____

Journal *(Continued)*

Journal *(Continued)*

Journal *(Continued)*

_____
_____
_____
_____
_____
_____
_____
_____
_____
_____
_____
_____
_____
_____
_____
_____
_____
_____
_____
_____
_____
_____
_____
_____
_____
_____
_____

Journal *(Continued)*

Journal *(Continued)*

Journal *(Continued)*

_____

_____

_____

_____

_____

_____

_____

_____

_____

_____

_____

_____

_____

_____

_____

_____

_____

_____

_____

_____

_____

_____

_____

_____

_____

_____

Journal *(Continued)*

Learn More

"Journaling has aided my healing and I hope that this journal may help guide you to greater healing from your own traumatic or difficult experience."

– Melissa B. Lombardo

It would be great to keep connecting via social media, Facebook, Instagram, and our website. You may use the hashtags #hurthealinghopebook and #writehealthrive.

Learn more at: **writehealthrive.com**.

Facebook: /Melissablombardoauthor

Instagram /Melissablombardoauthor

YouTube: /@MelissaBLombardoAuthor

Goodreads: goodreads.com/MelissaBLombardoauthor

Etsy: etsy.com/shop/WriteHealThrive

Meet Us

Melissa Lombardo

Melissa B. Lombardo is a CT State Certified Sexual Assault Crisis Advocate, speaker, and founder of Write, Heal, Thrive LLC. Her first book, "Hurt, Healing, and Hope: Thriving beyond Sexual Assault" is a book and performance piece delivering a collection of interwoven monologues detailing true stories of hurt and healing post-sexual assault, child abuse, domestic violence, and the after-effects. Each story, told from the first-person point of view, includes perspectives from healing allies offering support to survivors. "Write, Heal, Thrive: A Transformative Journaling Experience" and the "Write, Heal, Thrive Journaling Series" invites you to continue the nonlinear healing process of which journaling might become an additional tool for further reflection. For more information, visit melissablombardo.com.

Eduardo José Arias Cruz

Eduardo José Arias Cruz, Nicaraguan visual artist, art instructor, and graphic designer brings the healing journey to life through these original illustrations. For more information about Eduardo, visit eduardoariascruz.com.

.

www.ingramcontent.com/pod-product-compliance
Lightning Source LLC
Chambersburg PA
CBHW051636120626

46551CB00014B/2111